Summary & Analysis

ALEXANDER HAMILTON

Based on the Book
by Ron Chernow

WORTH BOOKS
SMART SUMMARIES

This Worth Books book is based on the 2004 paperback edition of *Alexander Hamilton* by Ron Chernow published by Penguin.

ISBN: 978-1-5040-4666-4

Worth Books
180 Maiden Lane
Suite 8A
New York, NY 10038
www.worthbooks.com

WORTH BOOKS
SMART SUMMARIES

Worth Books is a division of Open Road Integrated Media, Inc.

Contents

Context

Ron Chernow was already a widely respected historian and biographer, having explored the lives of important figures in politics and business, including George Washington, J. P. Morgan, the Warburgs, and John D. Rockefeller, so it is no surprise that *Alexander Hamilton* landed on the *New York Times* hardcover nonfiction bestseller list in May 2004, weeks after it was published.

George W. Bush was president, and less than three years had passed since the September 11 terrorist attacks in New York and Pennsylvania. Interest in Hamilton may have been spurred, in part, by a fresh controversy buzzing around his chief political rival, Thomas Jefferson, which began in the late

1990s. In 1997, *Thomas Jefferson and Sally Hemings: An American Controversy* by Annette Gordon-Reed was published. This work explored the longstanding rumor that Jefferson had fathered children with his slave Sally Hemings; a subsequent DNA analysis confirmed that he had. Among its many effects, this revelation provoked a reexamination of the founding fathers. Because Hamilton was in so many ways the antithesis of Jefferson—self-made, antislavery, pro-city—he was poised to attract new attention.

Though not an absolute dearth of biographies on Alexander Hamilton—there was Richard Brookhiser's *Alexander Hamilton, American* (1999), Willard Sterne Randall's *Alexander Hamilton: A Life* (2003), and some others—the time was right for Ron Chernow to turn his eye to Hamilton and tell this story.

In a 2013 interview with Biographers International Organization, Chernow spoke of hearing fans at a lecture shout out names of possible subjects for the book he'd write after *Titan: The Life of John D. Rockefeller Sr.*: "Alexander Hamilton was the perfect transitional figure for my next book, because there would be financial history galore while also opening up vast new subjects for study: military history, constitutional law, foreign policy, and dozens of other topics."

When Charlie Rose asked, in 2016, about the origins of this biography, Chernow said, "Hamilton was the neglected and misunderstood founding father."

Having been impressed by the dramatic arc of Alexander Hamilton's life—from his humble and tragic beginnings in St. Croix to his great achievements as a soldier, administrator, economic and foreign policy theorist, lawyer, writer, and entrepreneur—Chernow turned his focus to this work of tremendous scholarship.

Though almost anyone can appreciate a good "pulling one's self up by their own bootstraps story," Hamilton's foresight and business prowess are of particular interest to readers today who are concerned with interpretations of the Constitution, the state of the US banking industry, the power of Wall Street, and global economics.

The Impact on Culture and Currency

The indelible mark *Alexander Hamilton* has left on culture owes some acknowledgment to Lin-Manuel Miranda.

Ron Chernow's dramatic only-in-America biography of Alexander Hamilton caught the eye of the acclaimed playwright Lin-Manuel Miranda. In consultation with Chernow, Miranda crafted a genre-breaking musical drama based on Hamilton's life that cast predominately minority actors and featured songs in hip-hop verse. The musical has been a critical and popular smash, and has effectively elevated Hamilton to America's most popular founding father, and helped to bring Ron Chernow's study to the top of the *New York Times* paperback bestseller list in 2015.

And what of the ten-dollar bill? John Trumbull's portrait of Alexander Hamilton's has graced the front (obverse) side of the $10 bill since 1861, but in 2015, Treasury Secretary Jack Lew made an announcement: "the new $10 bill will be the first bill in more than a century to feature the portrait of a woman." To go into circulation in time for the 100th anniversary of women having the right to vote, the new design would feature Alexander Hamilton *and* the female finalist, Harriet Tubman.

Though mainly applauded from coast to coast, this initiative was not without controversy. Many suggested that replacing Andrew Jackson on the $20 would be a greater expression of justice, since he was a known slaveholder, responsible for the Indian Removal Act.

Could the "super-fans" dedicated to all things Hamilton, including Ron Chernow's remarkable study of a great American leader, have had an influence on Lew's final 2016 decision? According to Politico, "While he explained that Hamilton was on the chopping block as a matter of practicality—the $10 bill was the next one up for a redesign—Lew still got an earful from fans of Hamilton, who helped create the Treasury Department and the modern American financial system."

Alexander Hamilton will remain on the $10 bill, and the rest is history.

Overview

Above all, *Alexander Hamilton* is an attempt to correct the record. Of all the founding fathers of the United States, Hamilton is probably the least familiar to most Americans. There are no legends about his involvement with a cherry tree, or commemorations of his lofty remarks on human liberty every July.

To those who are more familiar with Hamilton, the associations are usually mildly impressive at best, and negative at worst. In the popular imagination, he's typically recalled as either a creator of the Bank of New York, a symbol of central government overreach, or a foil to Thomas Jefferson. As Ron Chernow explains, Hamilton "seems trapped in a crude historical cartoon that pits 'Jeffersonian democracy' against 'Hamiltonian aristocracy.'"

And yet Hamilton had a starring role in every major event in early US history, from the Revolutionary War through the second Jefferson presidency. Far from being a secondary character, Hamilton was a bona fide crafter of the republic. His positions were so nuanced—he fought the British courageously in the Revolutionary War, yet defended Loyalists in his law practice after it ended, for example—any stock characterization crumbles under scrutiny.

That's what *Alexander Hamilton* is—a reexamination of conventional wisdom. Beginning with an archives-spanning investigation of Hamilton's controversial origins, the book takes an immersive look at the man who authored *The Federalist Papers*, fought in the Revolutionary War, crafted the nation's financial system, served as George Washington's right-hand man, and much, much more.

His story begins under circumstances inconceivable to the other founding fathers—highborn men with lineages to be boasted about at lavish dinner parties. Though Hamilton's father, James, was born in Scotland to a noble family, by the time he met Hamilton's mother, his prospects as a West Indian merchant had likely evaporated. Stuck on the island of St. Kitts, he met Rachel Faucette Lavien, who had also experienced a marked decline in fortune. Even more burdensome, she had been married before. Her vengeful husband would not give her a divorce—common for the time—so she took matters into her own hands—uncommon for the time—and escaped from her household. As a result, Alexander and his brother, James, were considered "illegitimate." If that wasn't enough, by the time Hamilton was a teenager, his father had left the family and his mother had died. Not the likeliest of beginnings for a bitter adversary of presidents two through five.

This background doesn't only humanize this giant of the republic; it helps explain his life. Hamilton was an insecure striver who spent his adulthood making up for the deprivations he felt so unworthy of in his youth. His reckless military bravado, constant political battles, founding of the Bank of the United States, running a high-powered legal practice, holding disdain for slavery—all of this can be traced back to his early days.

While it propelled his professional life forward, his insecurity was also his downfall. Had this otherwise brilliant intellect, a man who wielded the power of reason like a cannon, not succumbed to his vanity, he might have turned down the duel that would leave his children fatherless—his wife, a widow.

Such are the contradictions of Alexander Hamilton, an all-American man.

Summary

Chapter One: The Castaways

Alexander Hamilton was born in 1755. He was raised on various islands in the British West Indies, a center of the world sugar trade at the time, but the precise location of his birth remains a mystery. His father, James Hamilton, was the fourth child of a Scottish laird, and his mother, Rachel Faucette Lavien, was from a mixed English and French Huguenot family.

Because his mother was separated from her first husband (who would not grant her a divorce), from a legal and social standpoint, Hamilton is considered "illegitimate," a circumstance that is both a secret source of shame and arguably the major cause of his insatiable drive to succeed. Unique among the founding fathers, his childhood is beset by a nearly unimaginable number of tragedies and financial hardships.

Chapter Two: Hurricane

Despite his tumultuous upbringing, Hamilton is a remarkable student. A chance encounter with Hugh Knox, a fatherly Presbyterian minister who had recently relocated to the island of St. Croix, helps the precocious teenage Hamilton win sponsorship to study in North America. He leaves the island overwhelmed by the belief that he is, at last, fulfilling his destiny.

Chapter Three: The Collegian

After arriving in New York, Hamilton enrolls at the Elizabethtown Academy, a college preparatory school across the river in Elizabethtown (now Elizabeth), New Jersey. His connections in the West Indies put him into contact with members of the area elite, and he integrates himself into New York and New Jersey colonial society with remarkable speed and finesse.

Hamilton enrolls at King's College in lower Manhattan, which is overseen by a stern Tory president named Dr. Myles Cooper. Although New York is a

Loyalist stronghold, recent British actions against Massachusetts in response to the Boston Tea Party enrage many people in the city, and Hamilton is quickly sucked in to the bubbling subculture of anti-British activism.

Chapter Four: The Pen and the Sword

By April 1775, the political situation in New York had become explosive. After news of the deadly skirmishes at Lexington and Concord reached the city, newly formed militia groups begin rallying and harassing Loyalists, many of whom flee to England fearing for their lives. Hamilton immediately volunteers for service, but, despite his enthusiastic military participation and fiery rhetoric, he worries that unchecked revolutionary fever could lead right back to the kind of tyranny he is fighting against. He is soon made an artillery captain, and fights a number of major—and agonizingly bloody—battles in and around New York City.

Chapter Five: The Little Lion

All-out war erupts in the colonies. Hamilton demonstrates strategic talent in a number of retreats, and the leader of the fledgling Continental Army, General George Washington, takes notice of the gifted young captain. Washington recruits Hamilton to be one of his aides-de-camp, and Hamilton accepts the position, despite his wish—admitted years later—to be given a senior fighting appointment. Nevertheless, Hamilton predictably flourishes in his administrator role and earns enough of Washington's trust to serve as a largely autonomous representative of the general.

This kicks off a number of feuds, some of which would become lifelong, with various Continental Army military and political leaders unaccustomed to taking orders from a confident twenty-two-year-old.

Chapter Six: A Frenzy of Valor

Due to the unimaginable deprivation and death count at Valley Forge, the winter of 1778 marks the low point of Continental Army morale. In June, its fortunes take a dramatic turn. At the battle of Monmouth, with Washington's steely leadership—and Hamilton's intensity (or perhaps recklessness)—the Army inflicts significant casualties. With assistance from France, American victory slowly came to be seen as less than impossible.

Hamilton and his close friend John Laurens, an antislavery aristocrat from South Carolina, draft a proposal to abolish slavery by giving blacks freedom in exchange for military service. The proposal fails, leading Hamilton to conclude bitterly that, "prejudice and private interest will be antagonists too powerful for public spirit and public good."

Chapter Seven: The Lovesick Colonel

In 1780, the Continental Army endures another devastating winter while stationed in Morristown, New Jersey. Fortune turns, however, after a chance visit to Morristown by Elizabeth (Eliza) Schuyler, the beguiling twenty-two-year-old daughter of Philip Schuyler, a Continental Army general and one of the most distinguished figures in New York Dutch society.

Hamilton falls head over heels for Eliza. After only a month of courtship, the pair decide to wed; they marry that December. His frustration with Washington reaches a boiling point, and after being denied yet another request for combat, Hamilton resigns his position as Washington's right-hand man.

Chapter Eight: Glory

Even though he is no longer a member of Washington's staff, Hamilton continues to hound him for a military assignment. Washington finally relents, and, in the summer of 1781, Hamilton is put in charge of a light-infantry battalion. In September, he leads a courageous charge at the Battle of Yorktown that helps provoke the surrender of British General Cornwallis, a turning point in the war.

Chapter Nine: Raging Billows

Hamilton returns to the Schuyler family homestead in Albany, New York. Eliza gives birth to a son, Philip. After a brief period of domestic bliss, the new father resumes his frenzied life of writing, politicking, and arguing. He picks up the law studies he had begun at King's College and corresponds with the superintendent of finance, Robert Morris, about fiscal and monetary policy.

Morris convinces Hamilton to become a tax receiver for New York State. The state legislature is so impressed with Hamilton's performance that it chooses him, along with four others, to represent New York at the Continental Congress. After a punishing seven months trying (in vain) to make a case for a robust central government, he returns to New York City to practice law. He sets up his firm—and his young family—in a house on Wall Street.

Chapter Ten: A Grave, Silent, Strange Sort of Animal

Hamilton's law practice thrives. He takes on all sorts of clients—there was no shortage of legal disputes in chaotic, post–Revolutionary War New York—but comes to earn a reputation as a defender of Tories. Hamilton is appalled by what he considers the unfairly punitive actions of New York State against ex-Loyalists, and he insists reconciliation is not only proper, but prudent for the young republic. His long dream of a central bank comes closer to materializing with the opening of the Bank of New York in 1784.

Chapter Eleven: Ghosts

Hamilton and Eliza waste no time expanding their family; eventually they will have eight children. In addition to his legal work, Hamilton takes up numerous other causes. He helps create a Board of Regents for New York State and served as a trustee of his alma mater, King's College (now known as Columbia College), and joins an antislavery group called the New York Manumission Society.

Chapter Twelve: August and Respectable Assembly

After serving a one-year term in the New York Assembly, Hamilton is selected to represent the state (along with two others) at the Constitutional Convention in Philadelphia, which convenes in May 1787. The Convention's official agenda is merely to reform the failing Articles of Confederation, which earns it the reluctant approval of New York's populist governor George Clinton, a zealous advocate of "states' rights." After months of blistering discussion, however, the delegates emerge with an entirely new framework of governance: the Constitution.

Chapter Thirteen: Publius

As the specific details of the Constitution became available to the public, the country quickly splits into supporters ("federalists") and opponents ("antifederalists"). Hamilton believes that if he can just explain the logic behind the agreement, he can convert the masses to support it. Working with James Madison and John Jay, he published a series of eighty-five essays titled *The Federalist Papers* that make a case for the Constitution. They chose the pseudonym "Publius" for this venture, after Publius Valerius, known for overthrowing the monarchy and helping to set up the Roman Republic.

Chapter Fourteen: Putting the Machine in Motion

Given the deep divide over the Constitution, Hamilton understood that the new government had to be exemplary. Thus he pursued George Washington, who had come to take on mythical status, to run for president; the ex-general wins in a landslide. Robert Morris declined Washington's invitation to be Secretary of the Treasury, but recommends Hamilton, who accepts.

Chapter Fifteen: Villainous Business

Hamilton immediately gets to work laying the infrastructure of the country's financial system. With his typical intensity, he labors day and night researching and thinking about debt, bonds, customs accounting, and the like.

This culminates in yet another seminal work of analysis, *Report on Public Credit*, which he presents to Congress in January 1790. His recommendation to fund a meaty public debt causes a firestorm and is denounced by detractors—including his old ally James Madison—as a boon to speculators at the expense of the poor.

Chapter Sixteen: Dr. Pangloss

In March 1790, Thomas Jefferson, who had been serving in Paris as an American minister, arrives in New York to take up his post of secretary of state in George Washington's cabinet. Jefferson is horrified to learn of Hamilton's plan to have the central government assume the war debts of every state—a cornerstone of Hamilton's economic plan—and he joins James Madison in a rancorous opposition. In the end, the duo from Virginia agree to support Hamilton, under the condition that the country's permanent capital be built on the Potomac River.

Chapter Seventeen: The First Town in America

In the fall of 1790, the Washington administration moves to Philadelphia, the country's temporary capital. Hamilton quickly gets to work setting up customs regulations and a coast guard to enforce them. Insisting that the federal government needs additional sources of revenue, Hamilton proposes an excise tax on spirits; unsurprisingly, the measure faces stiff opposition from rural distillers.

Chapter Eighteen: Of Avarice and Enterprise

Hamilton's plan to charter a centralized financial institution, the Bank of the United States, provokes a showdown with Jefferson and Madison. For them— and many of the rural farmers in Virginia—banking is an evil, even treasonous, enterprise. In his defense, Alexander Hamilton invokes the necessary-and-proper clause of the Constitution, which, he argues, vests Congress with the power to generate revenue, thus creating the precedent for a liberal interpretation of the founding document.

Chapter Nineteen: City of the Future

Hamilton prevails against Jefferson and Madison, and the national bank is given its charter. In 1791, however, after a pregnant Eliza returns to Albany for the summer, he meets a twenty-three-year-old "maiden in distress" named Maria Reynolds. She speaks to him of an abusive husband and seeks his assistance. The two begin an affair that ultimately reveals itself to be a blackmail plot.

A panic erupts in the winter of 1792, implicating William Duer, a shady speculator Hamilton had been associated with. Government bond prices collapse, leading to a massive financial loss for bondholders. With no small amount of glee, Hamilton's critics accuse him—and the entire banking system he set up—of destroying the country.

Chapter Twenty: Corrupt Squadrons

The abiding hatred between Jefferson and Hamilton descends to new depths of ugliness. Jefferson hires the poet Philip Freneau to start a paper, the *National Gazette*, that is little more than a collection of editorials attacking Hamilton politically and personally; the paper eventually becomes the mouthpiece for the newly formed Republican political party.

Despite George Washington's pleas for a ceasefire, Hamilton strikes back with a batch of vicious editorials impugning the secretary of state.

Chapter Twenty-One: Exposure

Mrs. Reynolds and her "rascal" husband, James, continue their extortion of Hamilton. After an unlucky chain of events, the affair is discovered by a trio of Republican legislators that included Thomas Jefferson ally James Monroe. Confronted by the men in private, Hamilton confesses to the affair. The trio agree to secrecy, but, through Monroe, evidence of the affair leaks back to Jefferson.

Chapter Twenty-Two: Stabbed in the Dark

As George Washington ends his first term, the political death match between Jefferson and Hamilton continues with unabated ferocity; even George Washington, the American idol, gets caught in the crossfire. This polarization fuels the expansion of political parties, with followers of Jefferson increasingly organizing themselves into Republicans, and Hamilton supporters into Federalists.

Chapter Twenty-Three: Citizen Genêt

After Washington is sworn in for his second term as president in March 1793, revolution breaks out in France. As with everything else, positions on the conflict are seen as a litmus test of one's political philosophy: Jefferson supports it, while Hamilton, appalled by the revolutionaries' barbarism, denounces it.

The revolutionary government declares war on multiple European powers, and the cabinet convinces Washington to issue his Proclamation of Neutrality. The French minister to the United States, Citizen Genêt, angles for military and financial support for the cause, which would go against American foreign policy.

Exhausted by the constant battling and the president's perceived deference to Hamilton, Jefferson leaves the administration at the end of the year.

Chapter Twenty-Four: A Disagreeable Trade

In the summer of 1793, Alexander and Eliza Hamilton contract yellow fever. They are treated by Hamilton's boyhood friend Edward Stevens, now living in Philadelphia; Jefferson accuses Hamilton of hypochondria.

After he recovers, however, Hamilton faces a new threat: a Republican-led congressional committee investigating—again—his conduct in the Treasury

Department. Hamilton is exonerated, but the event convinces him that "no character, however upright, is a match for constantly reiterated attacks."

Chapter Twenty-Five: Seas of Blood

Despite America's declaration of neutrality, British warships begin seizing American merchant ships in the French West Indies in November 1793. The country is livid. To Republicans, this offered further proof of British deception—and the worthlessness of the (Federalist) policy not to support France. John Jay, now chief justice of the Supreme Court, was sent to England to negotiate on George Washington's behalf.

Chapter Twenty-Six: The Wicked Insurgents of the West

In the summer of 1794, grumbling among distillers over the federal tax on spirits erupts into a mass revolt in the mountains of western Pennsylvania. The tax is the federal government's second-largest source of revenue, but Hamilton—and eventually, Washington—perceives the revolt as a dangerous rejection of the Constitution and the authority of the national government.

Under Washington's orders, a consortium of militiamen from three states put down the insurrection, now known as the Whiskey Rebellion.

Chapter Twenty-Seven: Sugar Plums and Toys

In March 1795, the treaty John Jay had concluded with England reaches Philadelphia. Hamilton and Washington support it; though unfavorable in many ways, it preserves peace with the world's most powerful military and economy. It narrowly passes the Senate, but is not fully revealed to the public until July, whereupon it is, predictably, interpreted according to party affiliation.

Republicans are incensed at the deference paid to England, and demonstrations, some violent, break out in numerous cities to protest the treaty.

Chapter Twenty-Eight: Spare Cassius

George Washington shocks the nation with his announcement that he will not seek a third term. Federalist John Adams is elected president, and Jefferson, who received the second-highest tally of votes, becomes vice president.

Chapter Twenty-Nine: The Man in the Glass Bubble

In the interest of maintaining stability in the young, fractured nation, John Adams keeps the core of George Washington's cabinet on staff after he becomes president. In time, however, he begins to see this group as devious agents of Hamilton, whom he comes to despise for political and personal reasons.

Chapter Thirty: Flying Too Near the Sun

In June 1797, a series of articles appears in the press claiming to expose Hamilton's malfeasance as treasury secretary, which links his relationship with Maria Reynolds. Hamilton responds with a typically ferocious written attack, denying all charges of wrongdoing, but not the affair.

Chapter Thirty-One: An Instrument of Hell

The revolutionary government in France solidifies their power, and, in a show of opposition to the Jay Treaty, they authorize French privateers to seize American ships heading to Britain. This provokes a political crisis that, as always, divides the country by party: Jefferson and the Republicans favor canceling the Jay Treaty and reconciling with France, while the Federalists demand negotiations with the French government, and, if that doesn't work, a firm military response.

Chapter Thirty-Two: Reign of Witches

In an attempt to suppress brutal Republican dissent, the Federalist-controlled Congress (with the approval of John Adams) passes the deeply undemocratic Alien and Sedition Acts. Hamilton is initially critical of the measures, but in the end supports amended versions. The Alien Act gives the president the power to arbitrarily deport foreign-born residents, and the Sedition Act effectively makes it a crime to criticize the government.

In response, Thomas Jefferson and James Madison craft anonymous resolutions for the legislatures of Kentucky and Virginia that declare the acts unconstitutional.

Chapter Thirty-Three: Works Godly and Ungodly

Alexander Hamilton's father, James, who had been living on the island of St. Vincent, dies in June 1799. Hamilton had not seen his father in thirty-four years, but his island upbringing still seemed to affect his views, including those on slavery. In 1798, Hamilton had thrown himself back into his work with the New York Manumission Society, representing runaway slaves and advocating for abolition in New York State; in 1799, the Federalist-controlled legislature votes to gradually end the practice.

Chapter Thirty-Four: In an Evil Hour

Hamilton advocates for the funding of a beefed-up military to counter French threats, but after initial support President Adams unexpectedly changes his mind and elects to restart negotiations.

The reversal causes a permanent rift in the relationship between the men. Yet another blow—both emotional and political—came with the death of his longtime patron and friend George Washington in December 1799.

Chapter Thirty-Five: Gusts of Passion

In a display of breathtaking political chicanery, fellow New York lawyer and politician Aaron Burr engineers a Republican takeover of the state legislature, a move that culminates in his nomination for vice president under Jefferson.

Believing Adams has no chance of defeating this North–South alliance, Hamilton throws his energy into supporting the South Carolina Federalist Charles Cotesworth Pinckney for president, angering Adams even more.

Chapter Thirty-Six: In a Very Belligerent Humor

Hamilton's rage at Adams's slurs denigrating his conduct and character drive him to publish the *Letter from Alexander Hamilton, Concerning the Public Conduct and Character of John Adams, Esq. President of the United States*, a manic screed that likely does more damage to his own reputation than the President's.

In part because of the Federalists' internal discord, Jefferson and Burr win the 1800 election, gaining seventy-three electoral votes each.

Chapter Thirty-Seven: Deadlock

The Constitution had no provisions for resolving a tie in electoral votes, so it goes to Congress for review. Remarkably, Hamilton throws his support to his old enemy Jefferson. He believes that Burr is hopelessly unprincipled and he predicts (accurately) that Jefferson's anti-executive stance will diminish once he assumes presidential power for himself.

As Congressional electors debate the stalemate in their new home on the Potomac, Delaware Federalist James A. Bayard negotiates with Jefferson's representatives. In exchange for preserving central Federalist programs such as the financial system, Jefferson earns his tie-breaking votes.

Chapter Thirty-Eight: A World Full of Folly

After Thomas Jefferson's presidential inauguration, Hamilton largely retreats from public life, and in 1802 he completes a country house in Harlem Heights known as the Grange. He spends his days doting on his family and making up for his long absences. Around this time, however, tragedy strikes: The Hamiltons' oldest son, twenty-year-old Philip, is killed in a duel with a young Republican lawyer.

Chapter Thirty-Nine: Pamphlet Wars

Having no more use for Aaron Burr, Jefferson shuts his vice president out of his administration, and Burr secretly defects to the Federalist camp. Hamilton remains wary of his shape-shifting old New York colleague, but sees in him an opportunity to weaken Jefferson.

The ever-scandalous press—which was wielded more as an instrument of partisan warfare than institutional watchdog—reveals Jefferson's relationship with one of his slaves, Sally Hemings, to the public.

Chapter Forty: The Price of Truth

Disinvited from the next Jefferson administration, Aaron Burr sets his sights on the New York governorship. Hamilton worries that—if elected—Burr will join the burgeoning secessionist movement seeking to create a confederacy of northern states.

Though his influence has waned considerably, Hamilton reluctantly campaigns for the Republican candidate, Morgan Lewis, who wins the election by a landslide. Convinced that Hamilton has sabotaged him yet again, Burr nurses "a murderous rage" toward the aging Federalist.

Chapter Forty-One: A Despicable Opinion

As Burr grows politically isolated, his sensitivity to Hamilton's perceived disrespect festers. After disparaging remarks Hamilton made about him at a dinner party show up in the press, Burr can take no more, and challenges his foe to a duel. The honor-obsessed Hamilton accepts. The duel would be fought on July 11, 1804.

Chapter Forty-Two: Fatal Errand

Hamilton resolves not to fire his first shot at Burr, suggesting that he hoped the dispute could be settled without bloodshed. Still, in the lead-up to the duel, he takes great care to get his personal affairs in order. The two men meet in the early morning in Weehawken, New Jersey, across the river from New York City.

Who fired first remains disputed, but Hamilton's shot lands in a nearby tree, whereas Burr's enters Hamilton's abdomen. Bleeding and paralyzed, Hamilton is rushed to the Manhattan home of his friend William Bayard. He dies the next day.

Chapter Forty-Three: The Melting Scene

Alexander Hamilton's death plunges the entire city of New York into mourning. The state of New York brings murder charges against Aaron Burr, prompting him to flee south—but not before stopping in Washington to finish out his vice presidency.

He spends time among sympathizers in South Carolina, and then Europe, eventually returning to New York City after the charges against him are dropped. He dies in 1836, expiring in a hotel room in Staten Island, New York.

Epilogue: Eliza

Though absolutely devastated by the death of "her Hamilton," Eliza finds solace in her religious beliefs and her family. In her new role as head of the family, she pursues debts owed to Hamilton—such as his unclaimed Continental Army pension—and throws herself into two causes: promoting the New York

Orphan Asylum Society and safeguarding Hamilton's reputation.

By the mid-1800s she has become a living national treasure, regularly feted by presidents, ex-presidents, and other influential figures of the republic. In 1854, she dies at the age of ninety-seven in Washington, DC, where she had been living with her daughter Eliza.

Timeline

January 11, 1755: Alexander Hamilton is born in the West Indies. The exact location of his birth remains unknown.

1772 or 1773: Hamilton sails to North America. Soon after arriving, he enrolls in Elizabethtown Academy, a preparatory school in Elizabethtown (now Elizabeth) New Jersey.

June 28, 1778: Hamilton fights under George Washington's command at the Battle of Monmouth in New Jersey.

December 14, 1780: Hamilton and Elizabeth (Eliza)

Schuyler are married at the Schuyler family mansion in Albany, New York.

May 18, 1787: Hamilton arrives in Philadelphia for the Constitutional Convention.

October 2, 1787: The first installment of *The Federalist Papers,* written by Alexander Hamilton, James Madison, and John Jay, is published under the pen name "Publius."

1789: George Washington begins his first term as President of the United States; Hamilton serves in his cabinet as Secretary of the Treasury.

Winter 1791: The Bank of the United States—the national bank proposed by Alexander Hamilton— receives a twenty-year charter from Congress.

Summer 1791: Hamilton has an affair with a married twenty-three-year-old named Maria Reynolds.

1797: Hamilton's affair with Maria Reynolds is exposed in the press.

1798: Under John Adams's presidency, Hamilton becomes inspector general, second-in-command under George Washington.

1799: George Washington dies.

Fall 1801: The Hamiltons' oldest son, Philip, is killed in a duel.

Fall 1803: Hamilton secretly supports the candidacy of Republican Morgan Lewis over Federalist Aaron Burr in the 1803 New York gubernatorial race.

July 11, 1804: Aaron Burr and Alexander Hamilton meet for a duel; Burr shoots Hamilton; he dies the next day.

September 14, 1836: Aaron Burr dies.

Cast of Characters

John Adams: Massachusetts Federalist, signer of the Declaration of Independence and the Constitution, second President of the United States, and by the early 1800s, avowed enemy of Alexander Hamilton.

Aaron Burr: New York politician and aristocrat, vice president in the first Jefferson administration, and the killer of Alexander Hamilton.

Elizabeth (Eliza) Schuyler Hamilton: Hamilton's wife; she was born into an upper-crust Hudson River family that claimed the distinguished New York Dutch families Van Cortlandts and Van Rensselaers as members.

James Hamilton (father): Alexander's father; the fourth child of a Scottish nobleman, he traveled to the Caribbean in the mid-1700s to seek his fortune.

James Hamilton (brother): Alexander Hamilton's younger brother; he worked as a carpenter and spent his life in the Caribbean, never seeing his brother again after he left for North America.

John Jay: Distinguished New York Federalist; delegate to the first and second Continental Congresses; contributor to *The Federalist Papers*; broker of the Jay Treaty, which maintained peace with Great Britain during its conflict with France; and friend of Alexander Hamilton.

Thomas Jefferson: Vice president of the United States under George Washington; third President of the United States; minister to France; author of the Declaration of Independence; leader of the Republican party; advocate of states' rights and opponent of centralized power; and archenemy of Alexander Hamilton.

Rachel Faucette Lavien: Alexander's mother; when Alexander was born, she was separated from her first husband, Peter Lavien, who would not grant her a divorce, thus making Alexander's birth "illegitimate" in the eyes of the law and colonial society.

James Madison: Virginia delegate to the Continental Congress and Constitutional Convention, co-contributor to *The Federalist Papers*, and close collaborator with Hamilton until 1791, when he aligned himself with Thomas Jefferson and the Republican Party.

James Monroe: Republican, Continental Congress delegate, Virginia Senator, minister to France, US president, and one of Hamilton's many enemies; Hamilton blamed Monroe for leaking the story of his affair.

Maria Reynolds: Married woman with whom Hamilton had an affair while he was living in Philadelphia, the temporary US capital.

Philip Schuyler: Alexander Hamilton's father-in-law; a wealthy aristocrat and member of New York's Dutch society, he was a Revolutionary War general and senator in the New York State Assembly and US Congress.

George Washington: First US President; commander of the Continental Army; Virginia Federalist; and lifelong mentor and friend to Alexander Hamilton.

Direct Quotes and Analysis

"In all probability, Alexander Hamilton is the foremost political figure in American history who never attained the presidency, yet he probably had a much deeper and more lasting impact than many who did."

Though he never led the nation from the White House, Alexander Hamilton had more influence on the United States than many who were elected president. Among the notable achievements of this founding father are: military service under George Washington, establishment of the financial system of the United States and the US Coast Guard and Customs Service, founding of the *New York Post*, founding the Bank of New York and the Bank of the United States, becoming the first Secretary of the Treasury, and these are just a few elements of his lasting legacy.

"If Jefferson provided the essential poetry of American political discourse, Hamilton established the prose of American statecraft."

Thomas Jefferson was able to express the optimism and idealism of America, but Hamilton, the "American prophet without peer," had the foresight to understand the direction America was going in, and he laid the groundwork for generations to come.

Chernow describes Hamilton as "a thinker and a doer," in contrast to Jefferson's "rosy agrarian rhetoric." For example, Thomas Jefferson is often cited as being an idealist who understood America to be a land of farms and rural communities, where Alexander Hamilton was a pragmatist and a man of vision who argued for a future of manufacturing to balance that of agriculture.

"Like other founding fathers, Hamilton inhabited two diametrically opposed worlds. There was the Olympian sphere of constitutional debate and dignified discourse—the way many prefer to remember these stately figures—and the gutter world of personal sniping, furtive machinations, and tabloid-style press attacks."

Alexander Hamilton was an eloquent, inspiring thinker, but he could also be a petty, angry person who could play in the muck with his enemies. Ron Chernow paints a very three-dimensional view of Hamilton by exposing some of his less-than-stately but altogether human choices.

"If Washington was the father of the country and Madison the father of the Constitution, then Alexander Hamilton was surely the father of the American government."

Hamilton created much of the basic infrastructure of the US government that remains in place today. Among his lasting legacy, he is acknowledged as having argued to empower a centralized federal government; he served as first Secretary of the Treasury under George Washington, where he established policies and practices that strengthened the country; and he was an emphatic supporter of the Constitution—and was instrumental in getting it ratified. "He helped to establish the rule of law and the culture of capitalism . . ." that are fundamental to the way America operates.

"The first great skeptic of American exceptionalism, [Hamilton] refused to believe that the country was exempt from the sober lessons of history."

Alexander Hamilton was a political realist whose experiences taught him that the United States, for all of its lofty ideals, was no less immune to turmoil than anywhere else. He is described not one to succumb to the hopeful rhetoric of Jefferson and others, but instead stuck by his own pragmatism and worldview that resonated with the understanding that Americans are no different from citizens of other nations.

Trivia

1. When Thomas Jefferson assumed the presidency, the federal bureaucracy had only 130 employees.

2. Aaron Burr and Alexander Hamilton attended the same high school: Elizabethtown Academy in New Jersey.

3. In 1978, a group of psychobiographers argued that Hamilton's participation in his fatal duel with Aaron Burr was motivated by a wish to commit suicide.

4. After Hamilton moved to his new family estate in the Harlem Heights area, it took him an hour and a half to commute the nine miles to his office in lower Manhattan.

5. Hamilton was having breakfast with Benedict Arnold when the British turncoat received a notice that one of his couriers had been arrested; Arnold fled the meeting in horror, leaving Hamilton in a state of wonder until Washington informed him about the ex-general's duplicity later in the day.

6. Ron Chernow became a historical consultant for Lin-Manuel Miranda's award-winning Broadway musical, *Hamilton*, making sure that the play was based on fact. Miranda said, "I feel like Hamilton chose me. He reached out of the Chernow book and grabbed me and wouldn't let me go until I told his story."

7. While serving as an aide to General George Washington, he was warmly referred to as "Ham" or "Hammie" by his fellow officers.

8. Alexander Hamilton founded the Bank of New York in June 1784. Its stock was the first to be traded on the New York Stock Exchange.

9. Celebrated historian Ron Chernow graduated from Yale College without taking any classes in history.

10. A 2016 Washington University study conducted by memory expert Henry L. Roediger III found that, "about 71 percent of Americans are fairly certain that Alexander Hamilton is among our nation's past presidents." Reminder: He was never president.

What's That Word?

Exceptionalism, American: The belief that the United States is inherently different than other nations, though not necessarily superior.

Federalists: Supporters of a strong national government with powers that supersede those of state governments.

The Federalist Papers: The name for the landmark series of eighty-five essays authored by Hamilton (with assistance from James Madison and John Jay) that argued for the adoption of the US Constitution.

Loyalist: An American colonist who remained loyal to England and supported the British.

Ratification: The official approving of a law; often by a vote.

Republicans: Supporters of a weak central government and in favor of strong state governments.

Tories: People who wanted the American colonies to remain part of the British Empire.

Whigs: Opponents of the British Crown and official British policy toward colonial America.

Whiskey Rebellion: Outrage expressed by farmers in Pennsylvania when an unpopular tax on American-produced whiskey was set in order to generate revenue for the government.

Critical Response

- A George Washington Book Prize winner
- A Biographers International Organization (BIO) Award winner
- A National Book Critics Circle Award finalist
- An American Library Association (ALA) Notable Books–Nonfiction finalist
- A #1 *New York Times* bestseller
- A *Wall Street Journal* bestseller
- A *Washington Post* bestseller

"Exhaustively researched and beautifully written, this eight-hundred-page volume tells us a great deal about the Founding Fathers and helps restore one of them to his rightful place in the pantheon."

—*The Christian Science Monitor*

"By far the best biography ever written about the man." —*The New York Times*

"Ron Chernow has produced an original, illuminating, and highly readable study of Alexander Hamilton that admirably introduces readers to Hamilton's personality and accomplishments. Chernow penetrates more deeply into the mysteries of Hamilton's origins and family life than any previous biographer." —*Foreign Affairs*

"Chernow disentangles Hamilton's life from the enduring political legend concocted by his opponents, who demonised him as a 'closet monarchist' and wannabe Caesar." —*The Guardian*

"Ron Chernow's masterpiece offers redemption for a man whose name was sullied by his enemies—Thomas Jefferson, John Adams, James Madison—long after he died." —*USA Today*

"Literate and full of engaging historical asides. By far the best of the many lives of Hamilton now in print, and a model of the biographer's art." —*Kirkus Reviews* (starred review)

"Chernow's achievement is to give us a biography commensurate with Hamilton's character. . . . This is a fine work that captures Hamilton's life with judiciousness and verve."

—*Publishers Weekly* (starred review)

"Ron Chernow's outstanding biography, [has] seized a favorable moment to make the strongest possible argument for the man and his policies. *Alexander Hamilton* is not only the longest and most comprehensive biography of its subject to appear in nearly fifty years. It is an impassioned defense and the most absorbing psychological portrait of him ever produced."

—*Commentary*

"*Alexander Hamilton* is thorough, admiring and sad—just what a big book on its subject should be. . . . Hamilton is coming back because, of all the Founders, he is most relevant to the way we live now. His problems are our problems; his solutions anticipate (usually more intelligently) the wisdom of think tanks and talk shows."

—*Los Angeles Times*

About Ron Chernow

The author of *Alexander Hamilton*, Ron Chernow, grew up in Brooklyn and Queens, and claims that his "passion for history began at the local library." He attended Yale College and Pembroke College, Cambridge, and became one of the country's most accomplished biographers and historians. As a journalist, he is a frequent contributor to the *New York Times* and the *Wall Street Journal*.

By the time he chronicled the life of Alexander Hamilton, he had already written biographies on John D. Rockefeller, the Warburg banking family, and J. P. Morgan.

In 2010, he authored a new biography on George Washington, which received the 2011 Pulitzer

Prize in the Best Biography or Autobiography category.

Celebrated actor and writer Lin-Manuel Miranda created a musical based on Chernow's biography, *Hamilton*, which debuted on Broadway in 2015. The production, which earned eleven Tony Awards, has been a commercial and critical smash.

When asked what makes a good biography, Ron Chernow said, "My ideal biography makes the person come alive to the point that if the person were suddenly resurrected and walked into the room, I would know exactly how she or he looked, sounded, talked, walked, and behaved."

For Your Information

Online

"10 Books for Fans of Lin-Manuel Miranda's *Hamilton*." EarlyBirdBooks.com

"Charlie Rose Interview with Ron Chernow." CharlieRose.com

"The Federalist Papers." Congress.gov

"Hamilton's America." PBS.org

"Hamilton Biographer Ron Chernow Finds New York's 'Quietest' Home." WSJ.com

"The Historian Behind the Broadway Blockbuster." YaleAlumniMagazine.com

"An Interview with Ron Chernow." NYHistory.org

"Q&A with Ron Chernow." C-SPAN.org

"Ron Chernow, 2013 BIO Award Winner, Talks About His Work." BiographersInternational.org

"Ron Chernow—Hamilton: From History to Drama, Roosevelt House Public Policy Institute at Hunter College." YouTube.com

"Ron Chernow: What Would Have Happened If Alexander Hamilton Lived." Time.com

"Talking History Podcast: Bryan Le Beau Is Joined by Ron Chernow." OAH.org

Books

The Age of Federalism: The Early American Republic, 1788–1800 by Stanley M. Elkins and Eric L. McKitric

Alexander Hamilton: A Biography by Forrest McDonald

Alexander Hamilton: The Life and Death That Changed a Nation by Michael Williams

Alexander Hamilton: Writings (Library of America) by Alexander Hamilton and Joanne B. Freeman

The American Experiment by James MacGregor Burns

Duel: Alexander Hamilton, Aaron Burr, and the Future of America by Thomas Fleming

Other Books by Ron Chernow

The Death of the Banker: The Decline and Fall of the Great Financial Dynasties and the Triumph of the Small Investor

*The House of Morgan: An American Banking Dynasty
    and the Rise of Modern Finance*
Titan: The Life of John D. Rockefeller, Sr.
*The Warburgs: The Twentieth-Century Odyssey of a
    Remarkable Jewish Family*
Washington: A Life

Bibliography

"Americans Recognize 'Past Presidents' Who Never Were, Study Finds." https://source.wustl.edu/2016/02/americans-recognize-past-presidents-never-study-finds/.

Chernow, Ron. *Alexander Hamilton.* New York: Penguin, 2004.

"Hamilton Biographer Ron Chernow Finds New York's 'Quietest' Home." *The Wall Street Journal,* accessed 31 October, 2016, http://www.wsj.com/articles/hamilton-biographer-ron-chernow-finds-new-yorks-quietest-home-1471963341.

"'Hamilton: The Revolution' Races Out of Bookstores, Echoing the Musical's Success." *The New York Times.* http://www.nytimes.com/2016/05/04

/books/hamilton-the-revolution-races-out-of-bookstores-echoing-the-musicals-success.html?_r=0.

"Tubman Replacing Jackson on the $20, Hamilton Spared." Politico, accessed 31 October, 2016, http://www.politico.com/story/2016/04/treasurys-lew-to-announce-hamilton-to-stay-on-10-bill-222204.

WORTH BOOKS

SMART SUMMARIES

So much to read,
so little time?

Explore summaries of bestselling
fiction and essential nonfiction
books on a variety of subjects,
including business, history, science,
lifestyle, and much more.

Visit the store at
www.ebookstore.worthbooks.com

MORE SMART SUMMARIES
FROM WORTH BOOKS

HISTORY

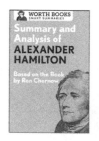

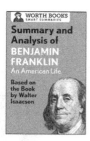

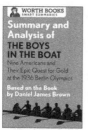

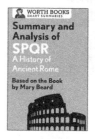

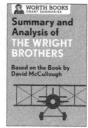

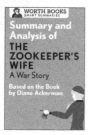

WORTH BOOKS
SMART SUMMARIES

MORE SMART SUMMARIES
FROM WORTH BOOKS

BIOGRAPHY AND MEMOIR

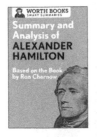

WORTH BOOKS
SMART SUMMARIES

MORE SMART SUMMARIES
FROM WORTH BOOKS

TRENDING

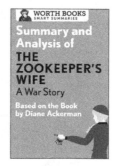

WORTH BOOKS
SMART SUMMARIES

INTEGRATED MEDIA

Find a full list of our authors and titles at www.openroadmedia.com

FOLLOW US
@OpenRoadMedia